WAR ROOM PRAYERS

Ways of communication and connecting to God
through prayers and supplication

BY

JAMES LANCASTER

TABLE OF CONTENTS

INTRODUCTION

War room prayers to heaven can be a strong wellspring of trust and strength in the existence of each devotee to Christ. Presently like never before, we can go to our Dad in Paradise to recuperate the hurt and torment that is surrounding us.

Have you at any point cried out to God out of vulnerability experiencing the same thing you were confronting? Life can appear to be really hopeless and defenseless now and again. It appears like haziness encompasses us every step of the way.

However, we should recall that we as adherents have the illumination of Christ living inside us.

We should let the radiance of God sparkle more splendid than any penetrating the murkiness.

We can do this through the force of petition.

Jesus previously crushed the foe on the cross, yet we actually wage profound fights every day while we are on this planet.

Jesus himself said this:

"In this world you will have trouble. But take heart! I have overcome the world." John 16:33

Assuming Jesus has conquered the world, that implies we are overcomers through him!

Now is the right time to stand up as individuals of God and utilize the weapon of petition to approach the name of the Master.

In this book we will see 9 strong war room petitions from Sacred writing that we can implore every day to prepare ourselves to take part in the fight that is happening around us in our present reality.

CHAPTER ONE

WHAT IS A WAR ROOM?

Many individuals know about the Kendrick siblings' film War Room that turned out in 2015 featuring Pricilla Shirer, T.C Stallings, and Karen Abercrombie. It is a film loaded up with trust and motivation as one lady frantically shouts to the Master in supplication. War Room has roused numerous Christians to develop their time spent in meditation by making their own "war rooms"- basically a spot in your home (generally a storeroom or confined place) where you can invest unified energy with God in petition.

WHAT IS A WAR ROOM PRAYER?

War room petitions to heaven can be any kind of supplication that you implore in your conflict room (you might even decide to make a request note pad or war fastener to sort out your requests). Petitions of request, mediation, acclaim and thanksgiving are incredible supplications to ask in your conflict room. I for one love to make war room petitions to God by utilizing Sacred text to direct my requests.

CHAPTER TWO

POWERFUL PRAYER POINTS TO PRAY

LORD SHOW ME YOUR GLORY

Then Moses said, "Now show me your glory."(Exodus 33:18)

In this entry Moses was addressing God in what was known as the tent of meeting. Anybody inquisitive of the lord would go to the tent of meeting outside the camp of the Israelites. It was here where God addressed Moses, as one addresses a companion (Exodus 33:11).

It was additionally in this gathering place where the presence of God was uncovered to Moses in a strong manner. Moses had the intensity to petition God and requested him to show him his brilliance.

Could you at any point envision what it probably was to prefer to view the strong brilliance and force of God? Since the sheer force of God's presence is a lot for any person, God permitted Moses to see his greatness cruise by, however he put Moses in the separated of a stone and covered his hand as he cruised by (Exodus 33:22-23).

Moses got a brief look at the awesome power and presence of God such that the vast majority didn't get to witness. When Moses descended from Mount Sinai after God gave him the Ten Rules, he didn't know that his face was brilliant on the grounds that he had spoken with the Ruler (Exodus 34:29).

What might occur if we somehow managed to invest energy with God in strong supplication to where our lives transmitted the adoration and force of God to everyone around us?

The word glory in Hebrew in Exodus 33:18 is kabowd, which means glory, honor, glorious, abundance, dignity, splendor, riches, reputation (source).Do we have the strength like Moses to petition God and request that he show us his

magnificence? To uncover to us his all-powerful

quality, wealth, honor, and strong overflow?

Astonishing things can happen when we strongly request that God uncover his magnificence to us!

War Room Supplication: Lord, I request that you show me your magnificence in a strong manner. I need to develop nearer to you and experience your sublime wonder and greatness. Like Moses, I want to meet with you and gain shrewdness and bearing from you. May the light of your affection and elegance sparkle upon me today. So be it.

CREATE IN ME A CLEAN HEART, OH LORD

Create in me a pure heart, O God, and renew a steadfast spirit within me.(Psalm 51:10)

There are times when we as a whole miss the mark, and need God's beauty and pardoning. David in psalm 51 submissively requested that God make a good nature inside him. Jesus arrived at this world and died on the cross so we can carry on with cleaned lives before God.

When the stains of sin seem to discourage you, remember the powerful truth and promise in 1 John 1:9,

Assuming we admit our wrongdoings, he is loyal and will forgive us of all our trespasses.

Acclaim God for the pardoning that we have through Christ! We don't need to live under judgment for our past sins, yet can stroll in truth, opportunity and triumph realizing that we are purged and refined of our wickedness, and we are perfect before Christ.

War Room Petition: Master, thank you that through Christ, I'm made clean. My transgressions that were once stained as red are currently all around as very white (Psalm 51:7). Like the song of David, I request that you keep on making a good nature inside me. Award me an ardent heart and soul that longings to do your will. So be it.

SAVE ME OH LORD

Save me, O God, for the waters have come up to my neck.I sink in the miry depths, where there is no foothold. I have come into the deep waters; the floods engulf me.(Psalm 69:1-2)

Have you at any point felt that life was challenging to such an extent that the waters and surges of your conditions appeared to take steps to take you under? Did you at some point feel like you were drowning and couldn't track down your balance?

In those snapshots of profound sadness and agony, we can reach our hands out to God and shout out to him, and request him to save us. He gives us timeless salvation through Christ, and can save us from the troublesome conditions we are carrying on throughout everyday life.

He can support us and put our feet on a strong stone!

"On Christ the strong stone I stand, any other ground is sinking sand, any other ground is sinking sand." (Song- My hope is Based on Nothing Less)

War Room Supplication: Lord, there are times when it seems like the preliminaries in my day to day existence immerse my spirit like a flood. In those minutes when I feel feeble and miserable, help me to remember your undaunted love for me. You are my Stone, and whom I stand. Much thanks to you Master, that you have saved me. So be it.

CHAPTER THREE

SUMMON YOUR POWER, O GOD; SHOW US YOUR STRENGTH

Summon your power, God show us your strength, our God, as you have done before. (Psalm 68:28)

We have power through Christ to do astonishing things for his realm. Before Jesus rose into paradise, he let the disciples know that they would be dressed with power from higher position (Luke 24:49). That power was through the astounding work of the Essence of God upon the arrival of Pentecost. As devotees, we have a similar Essence of God living inside us, who can do extremely and bountifully beyond what we can at any point ask, look for or envision in our lives!

War Room Supplication: Master, what a solace is to realize that I can track down my solidarity in you! You call forward your power and brilliance, and in my shortcoming, I'm made solid in you. Dress me with your power from a position of great authority, and outfit me with all that I want to carry on with this life for your honor and brilliance. So be it.

TEACH ME YOUR WAY, O LORD .

Teach me your way, Lord, that I may rely on your faithfulness; give me an undivided heart, that I may fear your name. (Psalm 86:11)

God is the best instructor isn'he? We can learn all that we want to carry on with an existence of righteousness and confidence in Him (2 Peter 1:3). His statement leads us as well as can show us how to live.

This is a request we can supplicate consistently, for God's Promise to show us his methodologies and not our methodologies.

War Room Supplication: Ruler, show me your methodologies. Show me and guide me on your way of affection, absolution, and elegance. Tell me the best way to stroll as indicated by your Promise

every day. So be it.

TEACH US TO NUMBER OUR DAYS

Teach us to number our days, that we may gain a heart of wisdom. (Psalm 90:12)

Life is short. There are such countless Sacred texts that confirm the way that our experience on this planet is transient. We can take full advantage of our experience on this planet by requesting that God train us to number our days.

Make the most of consistently.

We can't stand to squander a solitary day raging with outrage and sharpness now is the right time to exploit the time we have on this planet to have a strong effect on the world for the Realm!

War Room Supplication: Master, train me to number my days. Every one is a gift from you. Rather than investing valuable time and energy being consumed with stress, dread, outrage, and harshness, assist me with giving up my heart to you, and to observe the gift in every day you give. So be it.

CHAPTER FOUR

OPEN MY EYES

Open my eyes that I may see wonderful things in your law. (Psalm 119:18)

Have you at any point read entries from God's Promise that appeared to jump off of the page? The more we dive into his Promise, the more we can find valuable gems of shrewdness and understanding.

With the turn of each page, the brightness of these jewels has the ability to open our otherworldly eyes to find astounding insights. The more we invest energy in the Expression of God, the more wealth there are to reveal!

We can appeal to God consistently and request that he uncover the awesome things that he wants to show us through his Promise.

War Room Petition: Ruler, similar to the psalmist composed, open my profound eyes, so I might see magnificent things in your astonishing Word! Assist me with filling in shrewdness and understanding as I concentrate on your Sacred texts. So be it.

LORD, HELP MY UNBELIEF!

Mark 24, a man with a child moved by a devil moved toward Jesus for help. Indeed, Jesus disciples couldn't render a helping hand to this man's child (Mark 24:18). I'm certain this father was significantly deterred that his child kept on enduring brutally many years.

Yet, with a last amount of trust, he took his child to Jesus- - and watched what happened straightaway. The man submissively inquired,
But if you can do anything, take pity on us and help us." "'If you can'?" said Jesus. "Everything is possible for one who believes."

Then the dad offered something that we, at the end of the day, need to implore God consistently:

Quickly the kid's dad shouted, "I do accept; assistance me beat my unbelief!"

Isn't that the way in which we frequently feel?

We accept that God can do anything, yet we frequently question whether he'll follow through in our own lives. We know he can stroll on water and quiet the oceans, yet we some times keep thinking about whether he will meet our quick necessities when we approach him.

We need to accept that Jesus will act the hero, yet once in a while we think we are not qualified to get a forward leap from him.

In those moments of uncertainty, we can shout to God with a true heart. In Mark 24:25, Jesus drove the malevolent soul from the kid, and he was mended. We serve a powerful God!

War Room Petition: Ruler, I need to accept that you can assist me with correcting now experiencing the same thing. This situation around me appears to be so dreary and sad, however I accept that you are God All-powerful, and the sky is the limit for you. Help my unbelief today, and assist me with recalling that with you, everything is conceivable!

LORD, TEACH ME TO PRAY

In the Good news of Luke the disciples request that Jesus train them to pray. It is here when Jesus shows them the Lord's prayer.(Luke 11:1)
"'Our Father in heaven,

hallowed be your name,

your kingdom come,

your will be done,

on earth as it is in heaven.

Give us today our daily bread.

And forgive us our debts,

as we also have forgiven our debtors.

And lead us not into temptation,

but deliver us from the evil one.'"

The Lord's prayer is one of the strong petitions of Jesus we talk about in the Striking Supplications of Jesus Challenge. At the point when Jesus gives us direct guidance on the most proficient method to supplicate, we certainly need to focus.

Might it be said that you are once in a while adhered on what to ask? Let Jesus, our lord instructor, be our aide as we figure out how to approach him in supplication. There are times when we just might not have any words to say. However, when we approach God with a stance of lowliness, we are prepared to get from him, he will help us with what we want to say.

War Room Supplication: Father in paradise, I acclaim your blessed name. May your Life hereafter, and your will be done on earth for all intents and purposes in paradise. Today, I request that you give all my everyday necessities. If it's not too much trouble, pardon me of my wrongdoings, and excuse the people who have trespassed against me. Try not to allow me to fall into temptation , yet deliver me from the malicious one. May you get all the power, greatness, and distinction in my life-So be it!

CONCLUSION

Here are only a couple of supplications we can ask every day as we look for the Ruler and approach him in petition. God's Statement is loaded up with strong instances of petitions that moved heaven and earth, and we can approach the Master in supplication every day and move nearer to him with every request!